MORE SCIENCE SECRETS

Written by Judith Conaway
Illustrated by Renzo Barto

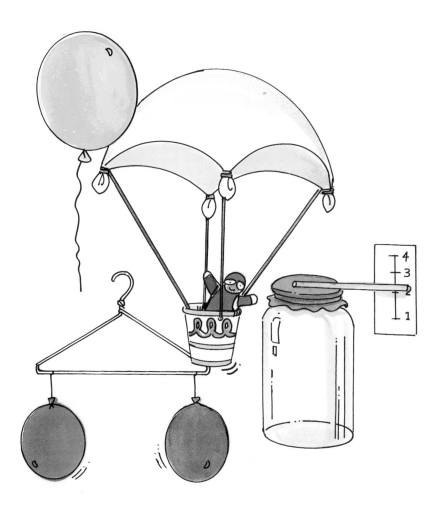

Troll Associates

Library of Congress Cataloging in Publication Data

Conaway, Judith (date)
   More science secrets.

      Summary: A book of experiments which prove basic
scientific principles including gravity, the
existence of air molecules, friction, and solar
power.
      1. Science—Experiments—Juvenile literature.
2. Physics—Experiments—Juvenile literature.
[1. Science—Experiments.   2. Physics—Experiments.
3. Experiments]   I. Barto, Renzo, ill.   II. Title.
Q164.C66   1987   507'.8   86-16084
ISBN 0-8167-0866-5 (lib. bdg.)
ISBN 0-8167-0867-3 (pbk.)

10   9   8   7   6   5   4   3   2   1

CONTENTS

GIVE YOURSELF AN IDEA

Science starts with ideas. With this science toy, you can give yourself an idea!

Here's what you need:

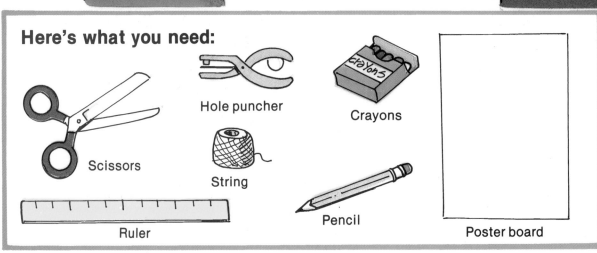

Scissors

Hole puncher

String

Crayons

Pencil

Ruler

Poster board

Here's what you do:

1 Cut a 2-½" × 3-½" rectangle out of poster board. Punch a hole on each side, as shown.

2 Draw your face on the lower half of the board. Flip the board over (top to bottom). Draw a light bulb on the top half.

3 Cut two pieces of string, each about 6" long. Thread a string through each hole, and tie two loops.

4 To give yourself an idea, hold the strings between your thumbs and forefingers. Roll the strings between your fingers until the threads twist. Then pull slightly to make the cardboard twirl. What do you see?

Here's what happens and why: You should see the light bulb appear above your head. That's because when your eye sees something, it remembers what it has seen. By twirling the card, you're making your eye remember two pictures at once. Your eye puts the two pictures together!

FOLLOW THAT BALL!

Because of a force called gravity, things pick up speed as they fall. This experiment proves it.

Here's what you need:

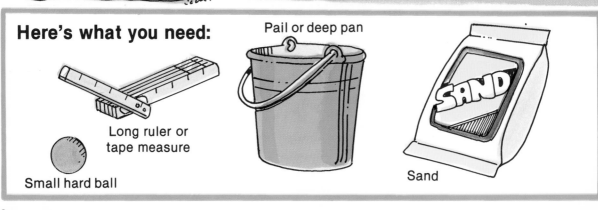

Long ruler or tape measure

Small hard ball

Pail or deep pan

Sand

Here's what you do:

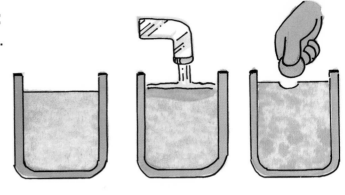

1 Fill a pail with sand. Add enough water so that a hard ball will leave a mark in the sand, when dropped into the pail.

2 Drop the ball into the sand mixture from a distance of 9 feet high. See how deep a hole the ball leaves.

3 Smooth out the sand. Now drop the ball from a place 6 feet high. See how deep a hole the ball leaves.

4 Smooth out the sand once again. Drop the ball from 3 feet. See how deep a hole the ball leaves now. Are all three holes the same depth? Which hole is deepest?

Here's what happens and why: The first hole should be the deepest. That's because the further something falls, the more speed it picks up. The ball dropped from the highest distance hits with more force because it is moving faster.

9 feet

6 feet

3 feet

WHIRLING GRAVITY BALL

Here's a fun experiment to do outdoors, where you have lots of open space.

Here's what you need:

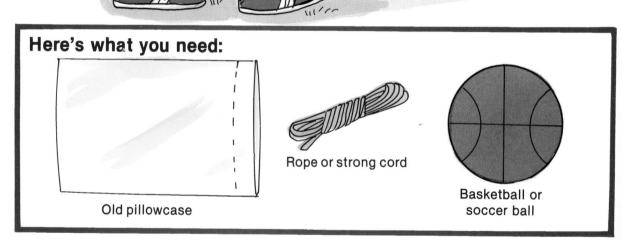

Old pillowcase

Rope or strong cord

Basketball or
soccer ball

Here's what you do:

1 Put the ball in the pillowcase. Tie a 5-foot-long rope around the pillowcase to hold the ball inside.

2 Now go outside where you have lots of open space. You're ready to see how the force called gravity holds the Earth in

place. Make believe the ball at the end of the rope is the Earth. Hold the other end of the rope in your hands. You are the sun.

3 Swing the ball around and around, in as large a circle as you can. As you swing the ball faster, can you feel it pulling on your arms?
This is something like the way the Earth moves around the sun.
But there is nothing tied to the Earth to hold it to the sun.
The Earth is held by the force of gravity.

4 Watch what would happen to the Earth if there were no gravity. Keep swinging the ball...then let go of the rope. Wow! Aren't you glad there's gravity?

HOW TO WEIGH AIR

When gravity pulls a thing down, we say the thing has *weight*. Everything on Earth has weight—even the air. Do this experiment to prove it.

Here's what you need:

Wire hanger

2 Balloons of the same size

Pushpin

String

Scissors

Here's what you do:

1 Blow up both balloons to the same size.

2 Cut two pieces of string of exactly the same length. Tie a string to each balloon. Tie the balloons to the ends of the hanger, as shown.

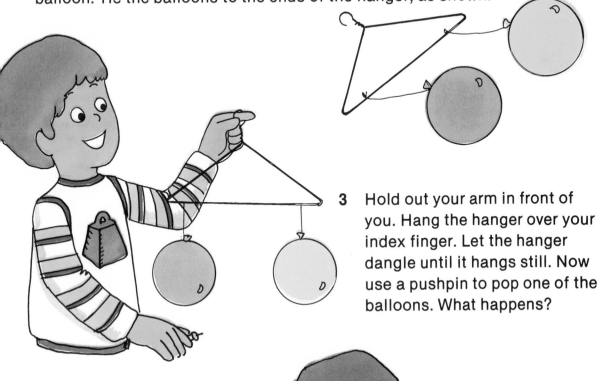

3 Hold out your arm in front of you. Hang the hanger over your index finger. Let the hanger dangle until it hangs still. Now use a pushpin to pop one of the balloons. What happens?

Here's what happens and why:
The side with the balloon full of air hangs lower. That means it weighs more. The only difference between the two balloons is that one is full of air. So you can see that air must have weight.

HOW TO DEFY GRAVITY

Gravity is a very strong force. Yet you *defy*, or go against, gravity every time you stand up. Trees and plants defy gravity every day. This experiment helps you find out how.

Here's what you need:

Stalk of celery

Red food coloring

Clear plastic cup

Water

Here's what you do:

1 Fill the cup about halfway with water. Add a few drops of food coloring, until the water is bright red.

2 Stand a stalk of celery in the water, as shown. Put the cup on a shelf, and leave it overnight.

3 Check the celery the next morning. What happened?

Here's what happens and why: The celery stem has turned red. The red water traveled *up* the celery stalk, against the force of gravity. How did it happen? The weight of the air pressed down on the water in the cup. Celery stalks are made up of hundreds of tiny tubes. The force of gravity pushed the water *down* and then *up* the tubes.

(There's another anti-gravity force at work here, too. To discover what it is, do the experiment on the next page.)

GRAVITY

UP, UP, AND AWAY!

In this experiment, you can see another anti-gravity force at work.

Here's what you need:

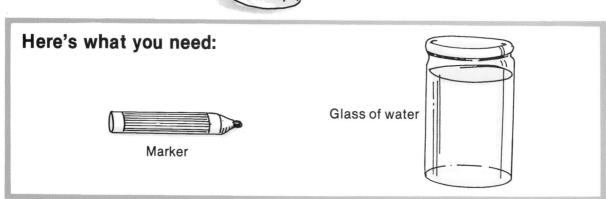

Marker

Glass of water

Here's what you do:

1 Fill a glass of water halfway. Mark the water level on the outside of the glass, using a marker.

2 Set the glass in a sunny window.

3 Wait at least two hours. Then mark the water level again. What has happened?

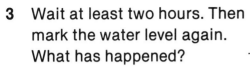

Here's what happens and why: The water level has gone down. Water is made of tiny parts called *molecules*. *Heat* is a force that can make water molecules rise against gravity. The force of heat pulled the water molecules out of the glass and into the air. That's why the water level went down. In the experiment on page 12, heat was also at work. While gravity was pushing the water down, heat in the air was pulling the water molecules up through the celery stalk's tubes.

MAGIC BOTTLES

This experiment shows how heat helps water to defy gravity. Do this activity in the kitchen sink, so you can clean up easily afterward.

Here's what you need:

Sink and running water

2 Bottles of the same size

Food coloring

4″ Square of cardboard

Here's what you do:

1 Put a few drops of food coloring in one bottle. Run the hot water until it is very warm. (Be very careful not to burn yourself.) Fill the bottle that has the food coloring in it to the top.

2 Run the cold water until it is very cool. Then fill the second bottle to the top.

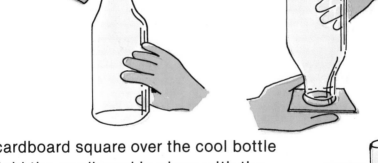

3 Place the cardboard square over the cool bottle of water. Hold the cardboard in place with the palm of one hand. Then, very carefully, turn the bottle upside down. Place it exactly on top of the warm bottle, with the cardboard in between.

4 Now hold the cool bottle by the neck. If a friend is helping you, have the friend do the holding. Then pull the cardboard straight out to the side. The necks of the two bottles should now be lined up and touching. What happens?

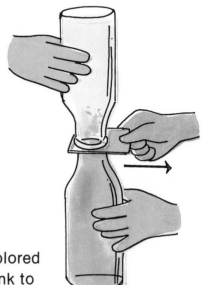

Here's what happens and why: Before your eyes, the colored water rose to the upper bottle. The cool, clear water sank to the bottom bottle. Heat makes water molecules rise. Cold makes the water molecules sink.

THE INCREDIBLE SHRINKING MOLECULES

Air is made of tiny parts called *molecules.* When you blow up a balloon, air molecules take up the space inside. You can make a full balloon get smaller, without letting the air molecules out. Here's how

Here's what you need:

3 Balloons

Tape measure

Marker

Pad

Pencil

Watch

Refrigerator

Here's what you do:

1   Use a marker to write a number on each balloon, as shown.

2   Blow up all three balloons. Tie them shut.

3   With a tape measure, measure the circumference (the widest part) of each balloon. Write the sizes in your pad.

4   Place balloon 1 outside the refrigerator. Place balloon 2 inside the freezer. Place balloon 3 on the lower shelf of the refrigerator. Shut the doors and wait thirty minutes.

5   Now measure the balloons again. Write the numbers in your pad, next to the first set of numbers. What has happened?

Here's what happens and why: Balloon 1 has stayed the same size. Balloons 2 and 3 have become smaller. Cold makes the air molecules *contract*, or come closer together. The colder it gets, the closer the molecules get. They take up less space inside the balloon—so the balloon shrinks.

DISCOVERING FRICTION

You've already learned about gravity and heat—two forces that move thing
Friction is a force that slows things down. These experiments can help you
watch friction at work.

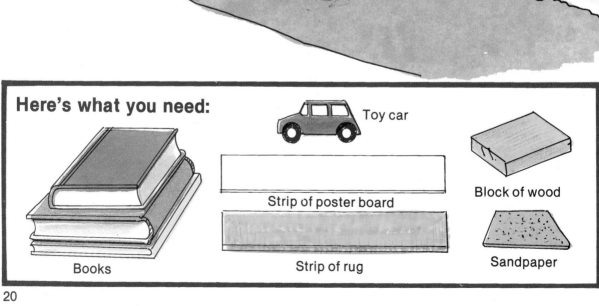

Here's what you need:

Toy car

Strip of poster board

Block of wood

Sandpaper

Books

Strip of rug

Here's what you do:

1 Stack several books on the floor. Then prop the strip of poster board against the books, as shown. Roll the car down the slope.

2 Next cover the poster board with the strip of carpet. Roll the car down again. What is the difference between the way the car rolled each time?

Here's what happens and why: Friction takes place when the molecules on one surface meet the molecules on another surface. How much friction happens depends on the kinds of surfaces. The poster board and the car's wheels are smooth, hard surfaces. So the molecules on the two surfaces slide by each other quickly. It's different when you use the rug. The rug has a rougher surface. The molecules of the rug reach out and "grab" the molecules of the wheels. The friction created is strong enough to slow the car down.

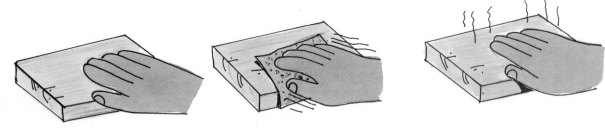

3 Now pick up a piece of wood and feel it. It should feel cool. Rub a piece of sandpaper back and forth over the wood. Then feel the wood again. It should now feel warm.

Here's what happens and why: The rubbing of the rough sandpaper against the wood creates strong friction. It is so strong that you can feel the heat of the reaction. Friction often creates heat this way. You use friction to make heat when you rub your hands together to keep them warm.

TOY PARACHUTE

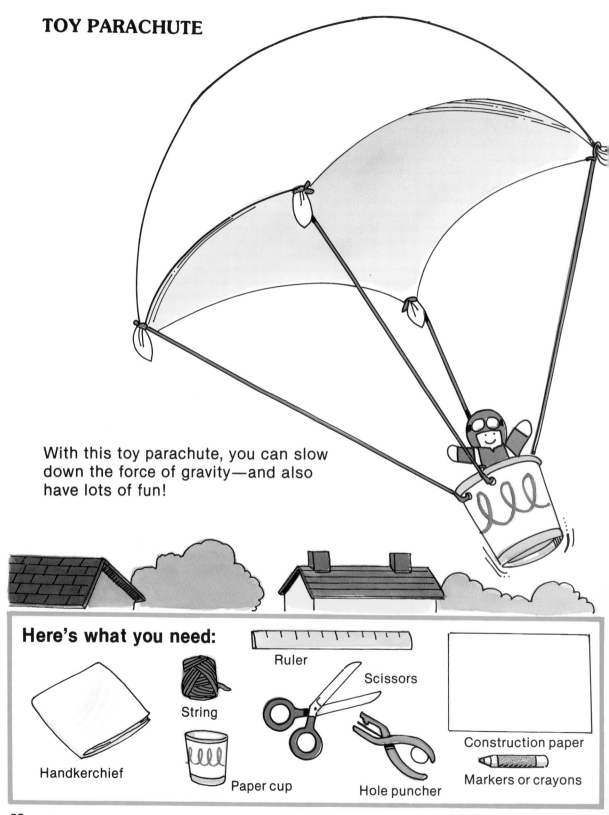

With this toy parachute, you can slow down the force of gravity—and also have lots of fun!

Here's what you need:

Handkerchief

String

Paper cup

Ruler

Scissors

Hole puncher

Construction paper

Markers or crayons

Here's what you do:

1   Punch four holes around the top of the paper cup.

2   Measure and cut four pieces of string, each about 20″ long. Tie a string to each corner of the handkerchief.

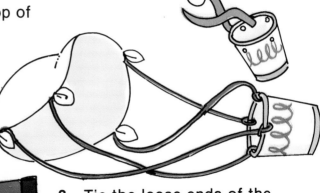

3   Tie the loose ends of the strings to the paper cup.

4   You can make some people to ride in your parachute. Copy the pattern shown here onto construction paper. Cut out the figure and color it with markers or crayons.

5   Now stand on a chair. Hold the parachute by the middle of the handkerchief. Put your "passenger" in the cup. Drop the parachute and watch it float to the ground.

6   Do some experiments with your parachute. First, drop the chute again, this time from a higher place. What happens? Next, have a friend stand under the parachute and blow up into the handkerchief as it drops. What changes?

Here's what happens and why: When you drop the parachute, air molecules get up under the handkerchief and react with the handkerchief's molecules, creating friction. This friction slows the handkerchief down. When you drop the parachute from a higher place, there is more time for friction to form. The parachute opens farther and takes more time to fall. When someone blows up into the handkerchief, you're creating more friction between the air and the handkerchief. So the chute takes longer to fall.

23

AIR-POWER BALLOON

Here is how to prove that air has power
when it moves.

Here's what you need:

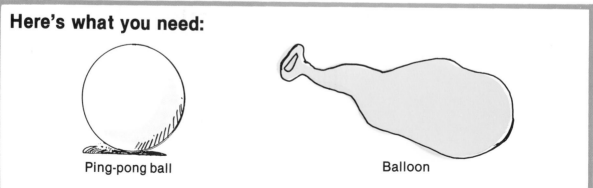

Ping-pong ball   Balloon

Here's what you do: **1** Blow up the balloon. Then pinch the end closed, like this.

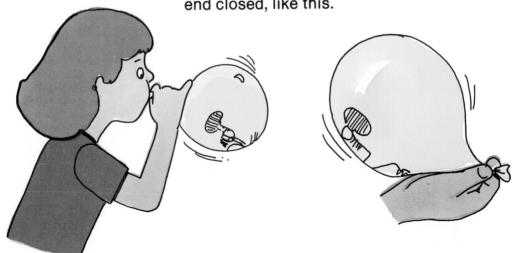

2 Now place a ping-pong ball on a table or floor. Put the end of the balloon next to the ball. Open your fingers just a bit, to let a little air out of the balloon at a time. What happens?

Here's what happens and why: The ping-pong ball moves! That's because the air outside the balloon pushes down on the balloon. The balloon then pushes against the air molecules inside it, forcing them out through the balloon's opening. The stream of moving air is strong enough to move the ball.

You can use air power to play an exciting game. Just turn the page to find out how.

AIR HOCKEY

Use air power—and have a blast!

Here's what you need:

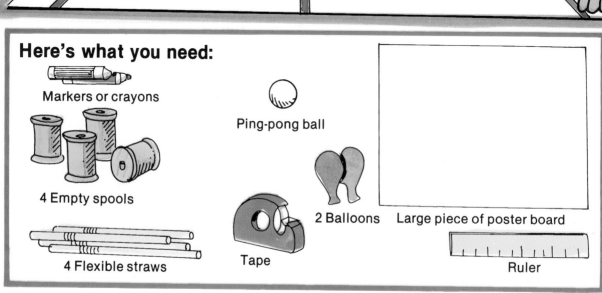

Markers or crayons

Ping-pong ball

4 Empty spools

2 Balloons

Large piece of poster board

4 Flexible straws

Tape

Ruler

Here's what you do:

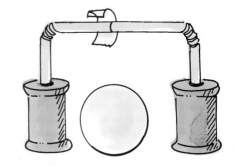

1　You will need to make a set of goal posts for each end of your playing field. For each set, use two spools and two straws. Put the short ends of two flexible straws into the holes of two spools. Join the long ends of the straws together with tape. (You will have to pinch the end of one straw to slide it into the end of the other straw.) Make sure your goal posts are wide enough for a ping-pong ball to roll between.

2　To make your playing field, measure the long side of the poster board, and mark the halfway point on each side. Then connect the two marks with your ruler and marker. This is the center line. Make another line about 3″ from each end of the board. To play the game, place the poster board on a floor or long table. Tape down the four corners. Set the goal posts on the two end lines, as shown.

Rules for Air Hockey: This is a game for two players. Each player chooses a set of goal posts. The object of the game is to score points by blowing the ball through the other player's goal posts, while keeping the other player from scoring. As the game begins, both players should be holding full balloons. Stand behind your goal posts, and keep the pinched end of your balloon at least 3″ away from the ball. Start the game with the ball in the middle of the center line. At the signal to go, start letting the air out of your balloon. Try to blow the ball toward the other player's goal. If you blow the ball out of bounds, the other player may place the ball on the edge of the field, at the last spot it left the board. The other player gets to shoot first. You may not touch the ball with anything but air from the balloon. When one player's balloon runs out of air, both players stop and refill their balloons. Then play begins again. *Scoring:* You get 5 points every time you make a goal. Play to 25 or 50 points.

BAROMETER

In weather science, the weight of air is called *air pressure*. Air pressure can be measured with a *barometer*. Here's how to make one.

Here's what you need:

Jar

Rubber band

Balloon

Notebook

Marker

Ruler

Scissors

Paper

Straw

Glue

Tape

Here's what you do:

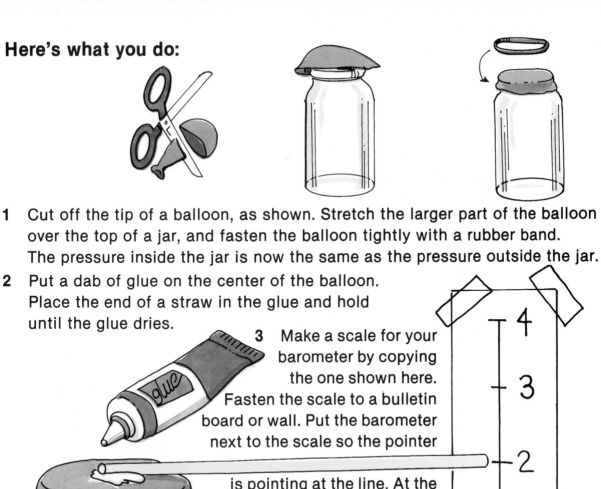

1 Cut off the tip of a balloon, as shown. Stretch the larger part of the balloon over the top of a jar, and fasten the balloon tightly with a rubber band. The pressure inside the jar is now the same as the pressure outside the jar.

2 Put a dab of glue on the center of the balloon. Place the end of a straw in the glue and hold until the glue dries.

3 Make a scale for your barometer by copying the one shown here. Fasten the scale to a bulletin board or wall. Put the barometer next to the scale so the pointer is pointing at the line. At the same time each day, write down the number the pointer points to. You'll see that from day to day, the pointer moves.

Here's what happens and why: When the air pressure outside the jar becomes greater, it presses on the balloon and makes the straw rise. When the pressure outside the jar becomes less, the air inside the jar pushes the balloon up, and the straw goes down. You can use your barometer to predict the weather! The air pressure is usually greater just before it rains. Air pressure goes down on dry days.

RAIN COLLECTOR

Here's what you need:

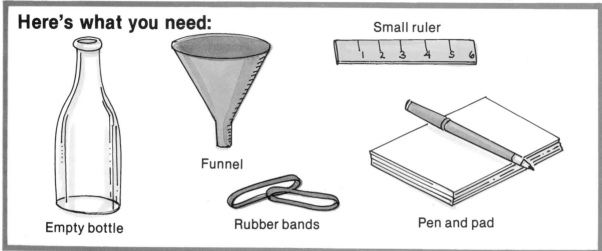

Empty bottle

Funnel

Rubber bands

Small ruler

Pen and pad

Here's what you do:

1 Use two rubber bands to strap a small ruler to the side of a bottle. Make sure the bottom of the ruler is lined up with the bottom of the bottle.

2 Set the funnel in the top of the bottle.

3 Place the rain collector outside. Each time it rains, note how many inches of water have fallen inside the bottle. Write the amount in your notebook. Then empty the bottle.

4 Notice the changes in rainfall from week to week. You and your friends can try to guess how much rain will fall each week. See who comes closest to guessing the right amount!

MAGIC BALLOON

In this experiment, you'll create electricity!

Here's what you need:

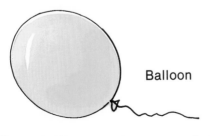

Balloon

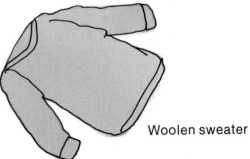

Woolen sweater

Here's what you do:

1 Blow up a balloon and tie it closed.

2 Now put on a woolen sweater. Rub the balloon against your sweater several times. Place the balloon against a wall—make sure the part of the balloon that rubbed against your sweater is touching the wall. Let the balloon go. What happens?

Here's what happens and why: The balloon sticks to the wall! When you rub the balloon against your sweater, you "charge up" the molecules of the balloon, creating electricity. Electricity causes the molecules of the balloon to attract the molecules in the wall. So the balloon clings to the wall.

MOLECULE MADNESS

Molecules make up everything on earth. When you mix two things together, you mix their molecules, too. Sometimes mixed molecules can have strange results! Do this experiment over the kitchen sink, so you can clean up easily afterward.

Here's what you need:

2 Jars

Baking soda

Measuring cup and water

Spoon

Vinegar

Here's what you do:

1   Pour about 1 cup of vinegar into one of the jars. Pour the same amount of water into the other jar.

2   Drop a spoonful of baking soda into each jar. Stir. What happens?

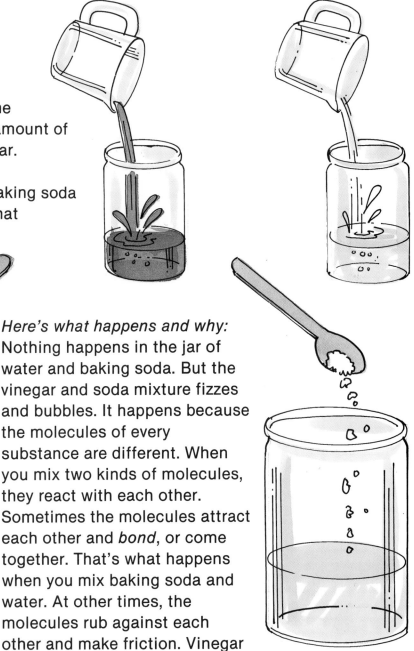

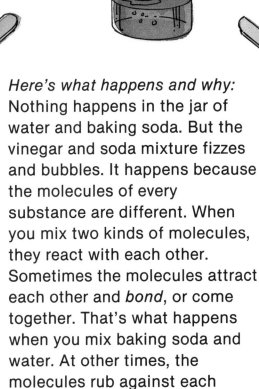

Here's what happens and why: Nothing happens in the jar of water and baking soda. But the vinegar and soda mixture fizzes and bubbles. It happens because the molecules of every substance are different. When you mix two kinds of molecules, they react with each other. Sometimes the molecules attract each other and *bond*, or come together. That's what happens when you mix baking soda and water. At other times, the molecules rub against each other and make friction. Vinegar and baking-soda molecules make so much friction that you can see the funny fizz!

SOLAR PINWHEEL

Here's a pretty way to see how the sun can make air move.

Here's what you need:

Small aluminum pie plate

Large aluminum pie plate

Small round mirror

Pencil with eraser

Pushpin

Scissors

Spool

A NICE SUNNY DAY

Here's what you do:

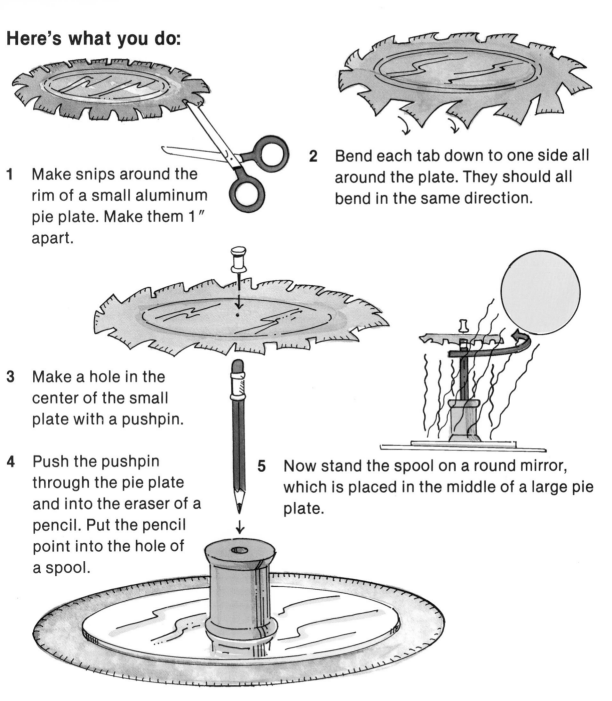

1 Make snips around the rim of a small aluminum pie plate. Make them 1″ apart.

2 Bend each tab down to one side all around the plate. They should all bend in the same direction.

3 Make a hole in the center of the small plate with a pushpin.

4 Push the pushpin through the pie plate and into the eraser of a pencil. Put the pencil point into the hole of a spool.

5 Now stand the spool on a round mirror, which is placed in the middle of a large pie plate.

6 Place your pinwheel on a flat surface where it will get direct sunlight. After several minutes your pinwheel will start to turn around!

Here's what happens and why: The sun's rays, bouncing back and forth between the mirror and the pie plate, create heat. The hot air rises and presses against the blades, causing them to turn.

SOLAR MITTENS

Even on a cold winter day, you can warm your face with these mittens.

Here's what you need:

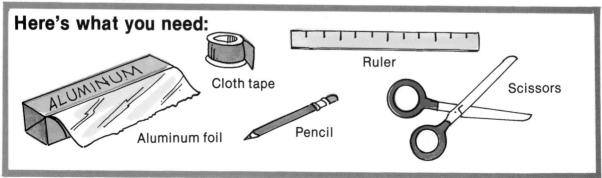

ALUMINUM

Aluminum foil

Cloth tape

Pencil

Ruler

Scissors

Here's what you do:

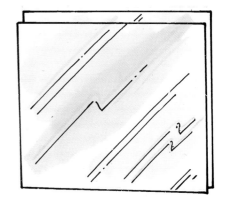

1 Tear off a length of foil (about 12″ × 24″), and fold it in half.

2 Trace two mitten shapes about 1-½″ away from your hands.

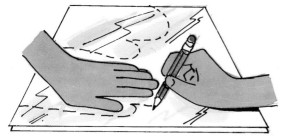

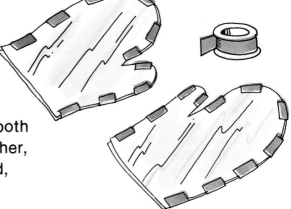

3 Cut out the mittens, cutting through both layers of foil. Keeping the layers together, use cloth tape to tape the sides closed, as shown.

4 Put the mittens on your hands and hold them so they reflect sunshine on your face. Feel the warmth?

Here's what happens and why: Heat and light from the sun travel in waves. The sun's waves hit the bright surface of the foil and bounce off toward your face. You can see the light and feel the warmth.

FLASHING SOLAR MOBILE

Hang this mobile in a sunny window and watch light flash around the room!

Here's what you need:

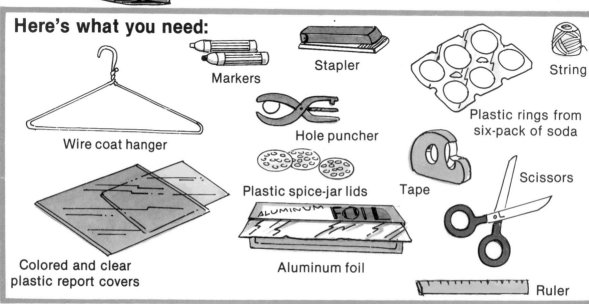

Wire coat hanger

Markers

Stapler

Hole puncher

Plastic spice-jar lids

Tape

Plastic rings from six-pack of soda

String

Scissors

Colored and clear plastic report covers

Aluminum foil

Ruler

Here's what you do:

1 Cut apart some plastic rings from the holder of a six-pack of soda.
2 Tape a length of string to a 4″ square of foil. Then crumple the foil. Tie the foil ball to the plastic rings. Use string to tie the rings to the hanger.

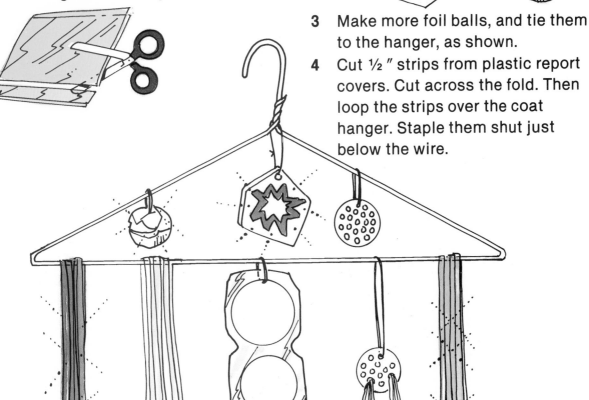

3 Make more foil balls, and tie them to the hanger, as shown.
4 Cut ½″ strips from plastic report covers. Cut across the fold. Then loop the strips over the coat hanger. Staple them shut just below the wire.

5 Tie a string to each of the plastic spice-jar lids, and attach them to the hanger.

6 Cut a piece of clear plastic report cover. Use markers to decorate it. Punch a hole in the plastic. Attach string to the hole and hang from the hanger.

7 Cut out long, thin strips of foil, each about ¼″ wide. Hang some over the hanger. Tie others to the plastic spice-jar lids.

8 Your mobile is ready to hang in a sunny window. Watch what happens!

Here's what happens and why: All the things on your mobile either reflect light waves or let light pass through them. The reflections cause little flickers of light to bounce off the walls. The light that passes through makes pools of color.

DANCING DOLLS

On page 32, you learned how to create electricity. Here's a fun game to play with that electricity!

Here's what you need:

Clear wrap

Markers

Pencil

Woolen cloth

4 Books

Scissors

Tracing paper

Here's what you do:

1 Trace this pattern onto tracing paper twice to make two dancing dolls. Cut out each dancer. Use markers to color your dancers.

2 Set up four books, as shown, leaving about 10″ of space between the two stacks.

3 Cut a piece of clear wrap long enough to wrap around the two top books. Place the two dancers under the wrap.

4 Now rub a woolen cloth back and forth on the stretched wrap.

5 Slowly raise the wrap and the two top books. Watch your dolls start to dance!

SUN TO GROW ON

The sun helps plants to grow. Here's how to see it happen.

Here's what you need:

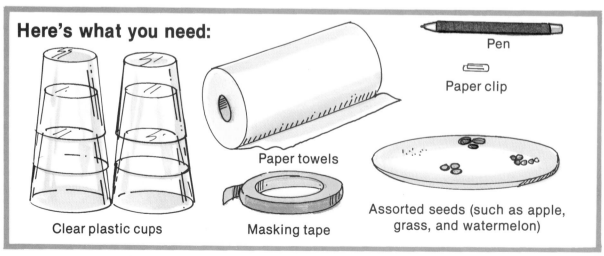

Clear plastic cups

Paper towels

Masking tape

Pen

Paper clip

Assorted seeds (such as apple, grass, and watermelon)

Here's what you do:

1 For each kind of seed you want to grow, you'll need two clear plastic cups.

2 Fold a piece of paper towel into a small square. Place it in the bottom of a cup.

3 Add enough water to soak the paper towel. Then put some seeds on top of the towel.

4 To make a roof for your small "greenhouse," turn another cup upside down and place it over the cup with the seeds in it. Fasten a piece of tape to the cups, as a hinge. Write the name of the seed on another strip of tape and attach it to the cup.

5 Set the cup in a sunny window. Keep your greenhouse closed most of the time. But watch closely—if it clouds up with too much water, prop open the top cup for a short time. Do this by slipping a paper clip onto the rim of the lower cup and letting the top cup lean on the clip.

6 Watch your seeds. You'll soon see them sprout into plants. You have created a small greenhouse. As sunlight gets trapped inside it, light and warmth are created, which help your seeds to grow.

WILDFLOWER GROWING CHART

Because you get energy from the food you eat, you are growing all the time. Use this chart to see how much you have grown.

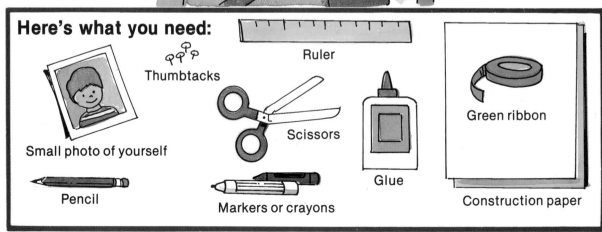

Here's what you need:

Small photo of yourself

Thumbtacks

Ruler

Scissors

Glue

Green ribbon

Pencil

Markers or crayons

Construction paper

Here's what you do:

1 Draw your favorite wildflower on a piece of construction paper. Color it with markers or crayons. Cut out the flower.

2 Glue a small photo of yourself to the front of the flower. After the glue dries, turn the flower over. Glue one end of a long green ribbon to the back of the flower shape. The ribbon is the stem of your flower.

3 Cut some grass out of a piece of green construction paper, as shown.

4 Stand with your back against a wall. Lay a ruler flat on the top of your head. Mark where the ruler touches the wall. Tack the flower to this spot.

5 Let the ribbon stem fall to the floor. Tack the grass to the wall in front of the ribbon. (The extra ribbon hides behind the grass.)

6 Measure yourself every month. Keep moving your flower up the wall, as you grow.

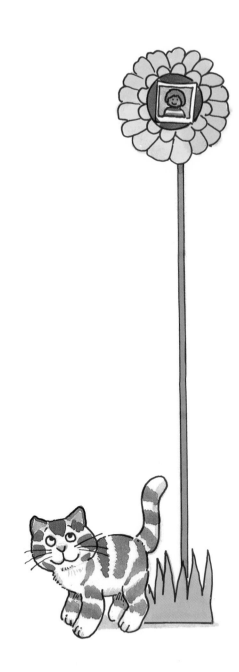